I0817191

ELECTRIC BUSES

Scott Wilken

Big Buddy Books
An Imprint of Abdo Publishing
abdobooks.com

abdobooks.com

Published by Abdo Publishing, a division of ABDO, PO Box 398166, Minneapolis, Minnesota 55439.

Printed in the United States of America, North Mankato, Minnesota
052023
092023

Design: Sarah DeYoung, Mighty Media, Inc.
Production: Mighty Media, Inc.
Editor: Katherine Chu
Cover Photograph: Mtattrain/Wikimedia Commons
Interior Photographs: aappp/Shutterstock Images, p. 21; Boston City Archives/Flickr, pp. 11, 28 (bottom); Ceri Breeze/iStockphoto, p. 15; Ian Dewar Photography/Shutterstock Images, pp. 17, 29 (bottom); iStockphoto, p. 7; liyuhan/Shutterstock Images, p. 27; Marcelo.mg.photos/Shutterstock Images, p. 9; Mtattrain/Wikimedia Commons, pp. 23, 29 (top); Picasa/Wikimedia Commons, pp. 12–13; Wangkun Jia/Shutterstock Images, pp. 19, 28–29 (top); wdstock/iStockphoto, p. 5; Windmemories/Wikimedia Commons, p. 25
Design Elements: octopusaga/Shutterstock Images (hexagon pattern); Vlad Malinovskij/Shutterstock Images (lightning bolt icon); Zoa.Arts/Shutterstock Images (lightning)

Library of Congress Control Number: 2022948821

Publisher's Cataloging-in-Publication Data
Names: Wilken, Scott, author.
Title: Electric buses / by Scott Wilken
Description: Minneapolis, Minnesota : Abdo Publishing, 2024 | Series: It's electric! | Includes online resources and index.
Identifiers: ISBN 9781098291532 (lib. bdg.) | ISBN 9781098277994 (ebook)
Subjects: LCSH: Buses, Electric--Juvenile literature. | Buses--Juvenile literature. | Electric vehicles--Juvenile literature. | Local transit--Juvenile literature. | Transportation--Juvenile literature.
Classification: DDC 388--dc23

CONTENTS

CHAPTER 1

SMOOTH & SILENT

Several people are waiting at a bus stop. The bus arrives almost silently. The doors slide open. Riders get on and off. The doors close, and the bus leaves as smoothly and quietly as it came. It leaves no smoke behind as it drives away. That's because it's an electric **vehicle** (EV)!

Many major US cities are promising to switch from gas buses to electric buses.

CHAPTER 2

WHY ELECTRIC?

Electric buses use a **motor** that is powered by electricity. There are many different types of electric buses.

Some electric buses get electricity from **rechargeable batteries**. Trolleybuses get electricity from power lines. And **fuel** cells are used to power newer electric buses.

Many schools are starting to use electric buses to protect children from health impacts created by burning fuel.

More communities are starting to use electric buses instead of gas-powered buses for a few reasons. Electric buses are better for Earth. Unlike gas buses, electric buses don't **release** harmful gases. And electric buses are quieter and can speed up more smoothly.

FAST FACT

German inventor Ernst Werner von Siemens built the first trolleybus in 1882. It was called the Elektromote.

Many scientists think that using electric buses is a way to lower air pollution.

CHAPTER 3

TROLLEYBUSES

The first electric buses were called trolleybuses. Trolleybuses are powered by electric wires above the streets. In the early 1900s, many cities in both Europe and the US established trolleybus systems.

FAST FACT

In the US, the first trolleybus routes were near Boston, Massachusetts, and Los Angeles, California.

The first trolleybuses in Boston were built by Pullman-Standard in 1936.

By the mid-1900s, most US cities used gas-powered buses. Gas buses cost less and were easier to use than trolleybuses. They didn't need to be connected to wires and could travel between cities.

Some cities still use trolleybuses. Seattle, Washington, has one of the largest trolleybus systems in the US. They use Xcelsior Trolley coaches made by the company New Flyer.

FAST FACT

Most gas-powered bus engines are called **diesel** engines because they use diesel **fuel**.

Xcelsior Trolley coaches have an electric drive system and batteries. They can even drive off-wire for a few miles.

XCELSIOR TROLLEY

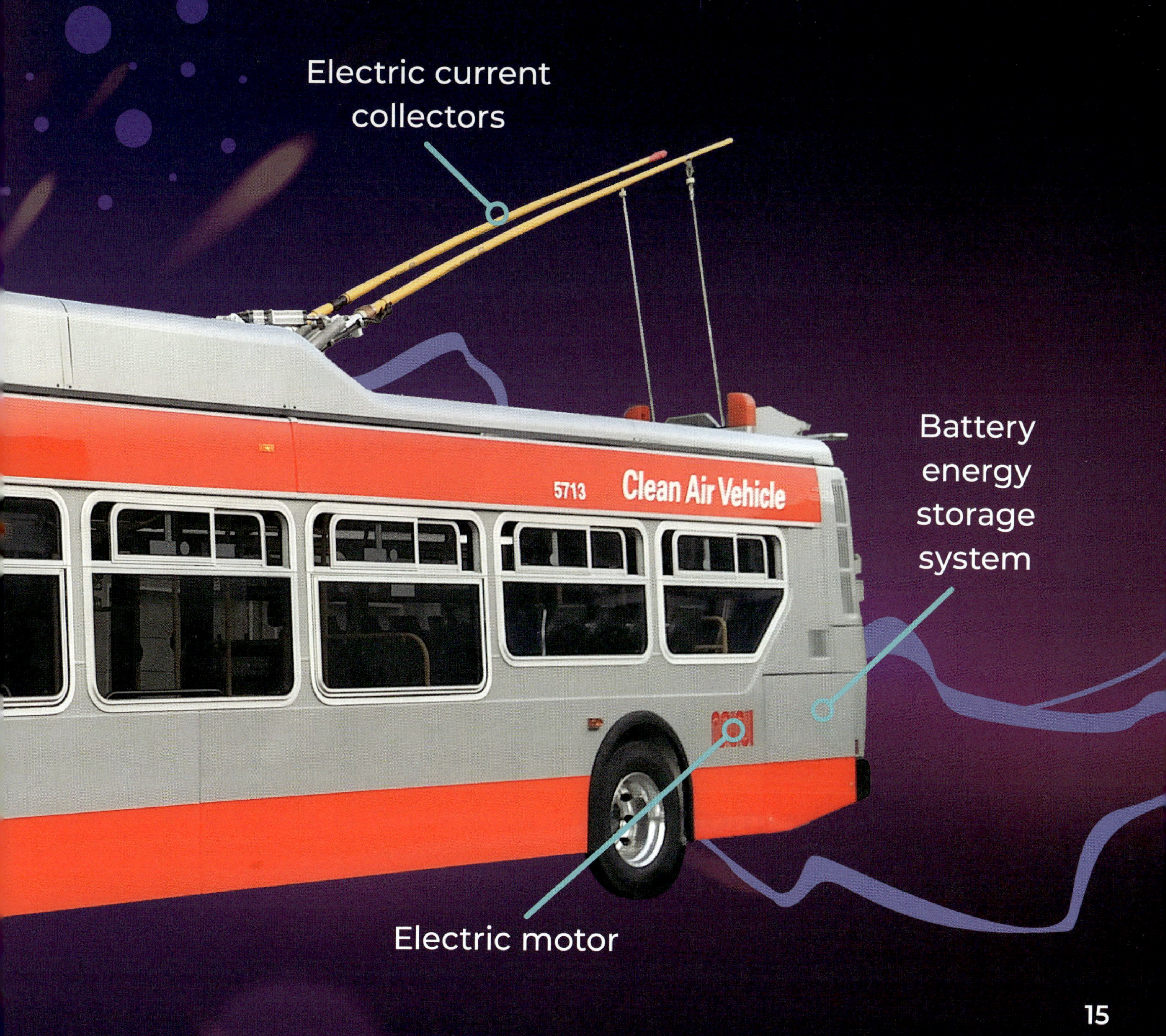
Electric current collectors
Battery energy storage system
5713
Clean Air Vehicle
Electric motor

CHAPTER 4

HYBRID BUSES

In the 1990s, some bus companies started building hybrid buses. Hybrids are powered by **diesel fuel** and electricity.

A hybrid bus has a diesel engine that creates electricity. It also uses **rechargeable batteries** to store the electricity. This electricity powers an electric **motor** that drives the bus.

Many hybrid buses require less maintenance and use less fuel than gas buses.

Many communities want to reduce **pollution**. Using hybrid buses in their public **transit** systems is one way to do this. In 2002, American bus company Gillig **released** its Low Floor hybrid bus. Cities across the country, including Buffalo, New York, and Maui, Hawaii, use Gillig hybrid buses.

FAST FACT

Gillig is based in California. It was established in 1890. Until the late 1970s, Gillig built mostly school buses.

Gillig started as a carriage and wagon shop in 1890. They started producing their first transit bus called the Gillig Phantom in 1980.

CHAPTER 5

BATTERY BUSES

Unlike hybrid buses, **battery**-powered electric buses only use electricity from **rechargeable** batteries. The batteries need to be charged when their electricity is used up. Some buses can be plugged into charging stations. Others stop under special charging bars that connect to the tops of the buses. This is known as **pantograph** charging.

Pantograph charging stations have many benefits. They charge buses faster and are easier to use than plug-in charging stations.

Canadian company New Flyer is a leader in electric bus manufacturing. It makes both hybrid and **battery** electric buses. In 2017, it **released** the Xcelsior CHARGE line of electric buses. These buses were made to be safe and better for the **environment**. Many **transit** systems in states such as New York, Utah, and Oregon use Xcelsior CHARGE buses.

New Flyer was founded in 1930. By 2022, it was one of the largest transit bus manufacturers in North America.

CHAPTER 6

FUEL CELL BUSES

The latest electric buses are powered by **fuel** cells. In a fuel cell, **hydrogen** and **oxygen react** to create electricity. A fuel cell is charged by being filled with hydrogen. Fuel cell buses can go about the same distance as gas-powered buses. And they don't need to be charged as often as **battery**-powered buses.

Fuel cell buses only release water vapor into the air. Water vapor is water in a gas state.

CHAPTER 7

THE FUTURE'S ELECTRIC

Many communities continue to add electric buses to their **transit** systems. Bus manufacturers also continue to improve electric buses and find new sources of power, such as **fuel** cells. This could help electric buses go farther and cost less. In the **future**, all buses could be electric!

Gillig is working to increase how far its buses can travel before recharging the batteries. And New Flyer is creating self-driving buses.

TIMELINE

1882
German inventor Ernst Werner von Siemens builds the Elektromote. It is the first trolleybus.

EARLY 1900s
Many cities establish trolleybus systems.

MID-1900s
Most US cities use gas-powered buses.

2002
Gillig **releases** its Low Floor hybrid bus.

2017
New Flyer releases the Xcelsior CHARGE bus line.

1990s
Bus companies start building hybrid buses.

GLOSSARY

battery—a small container filled with chemicals that makes electrical power.

diesel—a fuel designed for use in diesel engines.

environment—the natural world, including air, water, land, and animals.

fuel (FYOOL)—something that provides energy.

future (FYOO-chuhr)—a time that has not yet occurred.

hydrogen—a colorless gas that burns easily and is lighter than air. When hydrogen is mixed with oxygen, it forms water.

motor—a machine that produces motion or power for doing work.

oxygen—a colorless gas found in air and water.

pantograph—a foldable frame that transfers electricity to an electric vehicle from overhead wires or a charging station.

pollution—contamination of the air, water, or soil caused by man-made waste.

react—to go through a chemical or physical change.

recharge—to become charged again. Rechargeable means that something is able to be charged again.

release—to let go or make available to the public.

transit—the carrying of people, goods, or materials from one place to another.

vehicle—something used for carrying persons or large objects. Some examples of vehicles are cars, trucks, boats, and airplanes.

ONLINE RESOURCES

To learn more about electric buses, visit abdobooklinks.com. These links are routinely monitored and updated to provide the most current information available.

INDEX